Albertosaurus

Written by Frances Swann
Illustrated by Pam Mara

LIBRARY OF CONGRESS
Library of Congress
Cataloging-in-Publication Data

Swann, Frances, 1955–
   Albertosaurus / by Frances Swann.
     p.   cm. — (Dinosaur library)
   Summary: Follows Albertosaurus through a
typical day as the flesh-eating dinosaur hunts
and attacks other denizens of his prehistoric
world.
   ISBN 0-86592-527-5
   1. Albertosaurus—Juvenile literature. [1.
Albertosaurus. 2. Dinosaurs.] I. Title. II. Series.
QE862.S3S92 1988
567.9'7—dc 19   88-12118
                             CIP
                             AC

Rourke Enterprises, Inc.
Vero Beach, FL 32964

Quetzalcoatlus

Parasaurolphus

Deinosuchus

Corythasaurus

Spinosaurus

Oviraptor

Albertosaurus

Pachycephalosaurus

Anatosaurus

Struthiomimus

Scolosaurus

Rutiodon

Psittacosaurus

It was morning. Albertosaurus stirred drowsily. He had spent the night in the warm, dark shelter of a clump of willows on the flood plain. He looked out at the great green expanse of cattails glistening with dew. The plain seemed still and silent.

Albertosaurus had killed and eaten early the day before. Full, heavy and content, Albertosaurus had spent the rest of that day sleeping. Now he was very hungry again.

The willows hid his enormous frame well. Close by ran a trail to an crescent shaped lake used as a water hole by other animals. Albertosaurus had decided to lay in wait for them.

The sun rose slowly behind the long, thick, dark line of trees along the lake. Tiny biting insects buzzed around Albertosaurus and he shook his huge head irritably.

The movements disturbed a snake in the branches above him, and it slithered away. Albertosaurus waited impatiently. There were no signs of movement on the plain, but he watched a spider spinning a web among the rushes.

A little mammal jumped out of the undergrowth.
Albertosaurus made a half hearted lunge at it, but the creature
turned and fled at the first sign of movement.

Albertosaurus settled back to watch the plain. He was bored,
perhaps he would move on.

His gaze wandered over the plain. A gray shadow caught his attention. Suddenly alert and absolutely still, he watched as the gray patch grew larger and closer. Soon it was possible to make out a large herd of Triceratops. Albertosaurus could feel their great weight shaking the ground.

The herd closed in on his hiding place. Still he waited, his eyes searching for the weakest, most vulnerable animal. Then he saw it, a young female on the edge of the herd. Head down, and with a roar, Albertosaurus attacked. The shocked herd stopped and wheeled about to face Albertosaurus. His great teeth came down on the female's neck as she turned to defend herself. Her horns made contact with Albertosaurus, and tore at his thigh. Albertosaurus dropped back in pain.

The Triceratops stood, swaying slightly, blood dripping from her frill. Albertosaurus prepared to attack again, but a large male put himself between Albertosaurus and his quarry.

Other males had stationed themselves all around the edge of the herd. Albertosaurus was now faced with a defensive circle of heavily armored angry males. The male in front of him pawed the ground. Albertosaurus turned away. He had no wish to be charged at by an animal the same height as himself and much heavier. Roaring with frustration he retreated into the trees.

The herd moved on. Albertosaurus followed, hoping that the wounded Triceratops would fall behind and he could attack again.

His thigh ached and he was hungry. Then he stumbled. He had tripped over a Panoplosaurus.

Albertosaurus looked down. The Panoplosaurus lay clutching the marshy ground in terror. Albertosaurus tried to turn it over with his huge hind legs. He kicked and scratched at it, but the Panoplosaurus held fast, frantically digging its feet further into the earth.

Albertosaurus' claws made no impact whatever on its armored back, and eventually, shaking his head with annoyance he gave up.

Albertosaurus decided to head back to the lake, hoping to find possible prey there. Birds flapped up from the rushes as he approached, and in the distance a lone Stegoceras saw Albertosaurus. The lone Stegoceras turned and fled.

The lake was quiet and peaceful. Dragonflies darted low over the lily pads, and soft shelled turtles sunned themselves, occasionally dropping back into the water with a splash. Otherwise the lake was deserted.

Albertosaurus turned toward the river in the hope of finding a meal there.

The forest was dark and cool after the bright sunlight of the plain. Birds, disturbed by his presence fluttered above him, and the occasional lizard darted in and out among the tree trunks.

Albertosaurus pushed his way through the saplings and ferns, toward the river bank.

Suddenly he stopped. Albertosaurus listened. Above the noise of the river his sharp hearing had picked up the bellow of a Hadrosaurid. Here was another chance for a kill.

Albertosaurus set off along the bank, keeping a line of dense, tall rushes between him and the river. He drew level with the noise and stopped again.

He moved forward cautiously until he could see a herd of Saurolophus on a sand bar. They stood chewing conifer needles, unaware of his presence. Albertosaurus studied the herd, chose an elderly female, and attacked.

The herd turned in terror as Albertosaurus' huge bulk thundered across the sand. Bellowing, they threw themselves into the river and swam for their lives.

The old female was too slow. Albertosaurus lunged at her neck, his huge mouth wide open. She sank down under the impact, her long tail lashing desperately in the shallows. Albertosaurus closed his powerful jaws, and she lay still.

Albertosaurus stood over her triumphant, then he began tearing at the carcass. A pair of crocodiles, drawn by the smell of blood, scavanged at the tail.

Albertosaurus ate his fill. Then, heavy and content, he walked back to the bank. In a hollow among the rushes and lilies and in the shade of some sycamore trees, Albertosaurus lay down and slept.

The Skeleton of Albertosaurus compared in Size with a Man

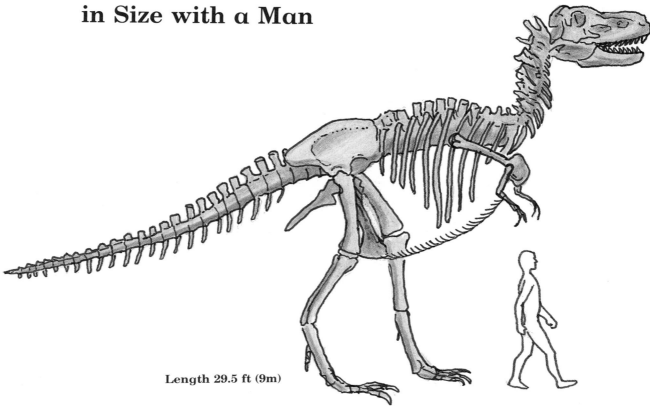

Length 29.5 ft (9m)

Albertosaurus and the Cretaceous World

The Age of the Dinasaurs

The word dinosaur is derived from two Greek words meaning "terrible lizard." All the dinosaurs lived in the Mesozoic era, 225 to 65 million years ago, at a time when the continents were much closer than today. At one time, much of the land was one giant continent called Pangea. This great mass broke up over many millions of years, and segments drifted apart to become our present day continents.

No man has ever seen a dinosaur – man did not appear on earth until a mere 2 to 3 million years ago. So how do we know so much about the dinosaurs?

Fossil Finds

Our knowledge comes from fossils which have been discovered all over the world. Fossil skeletons, eggs, nesting sites, tracks, dung, imprints of skin, and even mummified stomach contents have been found. New finds constantly update our view of the dinosaurs and their world.

When Albertosaurus lived

The Mesozic age is divided into three eras – the Triassic, Jurassic and Cretaceous. Albertosaurus lived at the end of the Cretaceous era, which lasted from 136 to 65 million years. The word Cretacious means "chalk." During this time great beds of chalk were formed, and the continents took on their present shapes. At the start of the Cretaceous era the weather was mild, but by the end it was much colder.

The land was low lying, and it was a time of high sea levels, with many deltas, rivers, lakes and swamps. Many new types of plants evolved during the Cretaceous period. Flowering plants appeared for the first time. By the end of the Cretaceous period many trees and plants had evolved which would be familiar to us today.

All about Albertosaurus

Albertosaurus was a tyrannosaurid dinosaur. The best known tyrannosaurid is Tyrannosaurus. Tyrannosaurus was 46 ft. long and weighed 7 tons. Albertosaurus was only 29.5 ft long and weighed 2 tons.

The tyrannosaurids were a fearsome family of meat eaters. They were powerfully built, with giant skulls, massive hind legs, and strong jaws. Their front legs were ridiculously small. These may have been useful during mating, or perhaps as a leverage when rising from the ground.

Albertosaurus was small and light for a tyrannosaurid. He would have ambushed his prey but been unable to chase it for any great distance. Large dinosaurs were too heavy to tackle, but the plentiful Hadrosaurids would have made easier prey.

Enormous jaws with rows of serrated teeth meant that Albertosaurus could slice through skin and meat, eating chunks of flesh and bone whole.

Fossils of Albertosaurus have been found in Alberta, Canada and Montana.

Other Dinosaurs in this book

All the dinosaurs in this book lived in North America in the late Cretaceous era.

TRICERATOPS

A 30 ft (9 m) long dinosaur that could weigh up to 5.4 tons Triceratops remains have been found all over North America. Triceratops was a short frilled Ceratopian dinosaur. It had three sharp facial horns. Under attack it may have charged its attacker in the same manner as our present day rhino. Triceratops was a plant eating dinosaur.

PANOPLOSAURUS

Panoplosaurus was a heavily armoured dinosaur. Only incomplete fossil skeletons have been found, but we do have well preserved skulls. Panoplosaurus was a plant eater. Under attack Panoplosaurus would have withdrawn its legs and clutched the ground, presenting a predator with only its armoured "shell".

STEGOCERAS

Stegoceras was a pachychephalosaur, or "thick headed reptile". This group of dinosaurs tended to live in upland areas in small herds, much as sheep and goats do today.

Stegoceras had a high domed, thick skull. Males probably fought for territories by head butting each other. Some sources believe that fossils with thicker domes were male. A fully grown Stegoceras was only 6.5 ft (2 M) long.

SAUROLOPHUS

A 30–40 ft long (9–12 m) hadrosaurid, or "duckbill" dinosaur. Saurolophus had an unusual bony ridge along the top of its nose with formed a spike on the top of its head. Different species had different shaped spikes.

The spike was probably used as a visual signal to others in the group, and as a resonator to produce a bellowing call. Saurolophus had a wide, deep tail and paddle like hands. Under attack it could escape a predator by swimming, as did the herd in the story.